WITCHES

BY JOHN HAMILTON

VISIT US AT
WWW.ABDOPUBLISHING.COM

Published by ABDO Publishing Company, 4940 Viking Drive, Suite 622, Edina, Minnesota 55435.

Printed in the United States.

Editor: John Hamilton
Graphic Design: Sue Hamilton
Cover Design: Neil Klinepier
Cover Illustration: *Witch Town* ©1977 Don Maitz
Interior Photos and Illustrations: p 1 Detail from *Black Cauldron* ©1976 Don Maitz; p 4 *Wizard of Oz* still, courtesy Metro-Goldwyn-Mayer; p 5 *Black Cauldron* ©1976 Don Maitz; p 6 *Snow White and the Seven Dwarfs* stills, courtesy Walt Disney Productions; p 7 Marian Anderson as Ulrica, Corbis; p 8 *Carrag the Black* ©1996 Don Maitz; p 9 *The Little Mermaid* still, courtesy Walt Disney Productions; pp 10-11 *Witch* ©1977 Don Maitz; p 11 Brothers Grimm *Hansel and Gretel*, Mary Evans; p 12 Gundestrup Cauldron, courtesy Australian National University; p 13 *Crone* ©1998 Don Maitz; p 14 Tollund Man, Corbis; p 15 Druid ceremony, Corbis; p 16 Arikara medicine man, Edward S. Curtis; p 17 Equador shaman, Getty; pp 18-19 Shortsy nation shaman, Getty; pp 20-21 Witch burning, Corbis; pp 22-23 *Witch Town* ©1977 Don Maitz; p 24 Mandrake illustration, Photo Researchers, Inc.; p 25 *Hocus Pocus* still, Corbis; p 26 *The Duckingstool*, Corbis; p 27 Witch Trial, Corbis; p 28 Fiona the Witch, courtesy the Sci Fi Channel; p 29 Modern witch, Corbis; p 31 *Witchcraft* ©1977 Don Maitz; p 32 *Mexican Sorcerer* ©1977 Don Maitz

Library of Congress Cataloging-in-Publication Data

Hamilton, John, 1959-
　　Witches / John Hamilton.
　　　　p. cm. -- (The world of horror)
　　Includes index.
　　ISBN-13: 978-1-59928-776-8
　　ISBN-10: 1-59928-776-5
　　1. Magic--Juvenile literature. 2. Druids and druidism--Juvenile literature. 3. Shamans--Juvenile literature. 4. Witches--Juvenile literature. I. Title.

BF1621.H36 2007
133.4'3--dc22

　　　　　　　　　　2006032741

CONTENTS

Witches & Warlocks.. 4

Those Bad, Evil Witches 6

The Mysterious Druids 12

Shamans... 16

Witches in the Middle Ages.............................. 21

Modern-Day Witches.. 28

Glossary 30

Index... 32

Witches & Warlocks

Below: A scene from the 1939 film *The Wizard of Oz.* Margaret Hamilton played the spell-casting, broomstick-riding Wicked Witch of the West. Judy Garland was the heroine Dorothy.

Witches, like those found in William Shakespeare's play *Macbeth*, are often portrayed as old crones, with warts and crooked teeth. They are evil, creepy old women with pointy hats who can see the future, or place curses on innocent people. In *Macbeth*, the three witches represent dark powers, an inner evil that influences people's minds. In their most famous scene, they prepare a potion that includes an eye of newt, a frog toe, bat's wool, and the tongue of a dog: "Double, double toil and trouble; Fire burn, and cauldron bubble."

In reality, not all witches are female. Men can be witches too, but they are usually called warlocks or wizards. And not all witches, even in literature, are evil. A few are good witches.

In the 1939 movie *The Wizard of Oz*, there is a good witch and a wicked witch. When a witch is good, it is sometimes said they use "white magic." An evil witch uses "black magic."

In this book we'll take a look at witches and how they are portrayed. Then we'll look at the history of witches, from Druids and shamans to the witches of the Middle Ages. Then we'll examine modern-day witches, who are definitely not old crones with warts and broomsticks!

Above: Black Cauldron by Don Maitz.

THOSE BAD, EVIL WITCHES

When you examine stories down through the ages, you can't read very much without bumping into witches. They are the favorite villains of numerous stories. For many authors, whenever their stories needed someone evil, they chose a witch.

A witch is often portrayed as a woman huddled over a ghastly steaming mixture in a big kettle. She tosses into the disgusting black liquid an eyeball of a reptile and the claw of a raven, and maybe a lock of human hair. She stirs the bubbling brew and mutters some magic words. And then something bad happens to the hero. Over and over, witches are portrayed as evil people who are somehow in league with the devil or demons. In these stories, witches have a variety of magical powers:

Curses and Spells

Witches can cast curses on people, giving them bad luck. Sometimes witches can place a curse or cast a spell with their own power. But for more difficult spells, they need to consult ancient books, and recite magical words. In the story *Snow White*, a witch put a curse on the princess so that she would sleep forever (or at least until a handsome prince came along). The placing of curses is seen most often with gypsies (now called "Roma"). Annoy a gypsy, and you might have seven years of bad luck.

Potions

Witches often put together some sort of mixture that makes people fall in love, makes them sick, or even makes them sleep forever. Oftentimes, to make the magic work, the witch needs an object, such as a lock of hair or a fingernail, from the person who is the target of the potion.

Below: The Evil Queen from Disney's *Snow White and the Seven Dwarfs* transforms herself into an old hag to give the lovely Snow White a poison apple.

Above: Singer Marian Anderson plays the fortune-teller Ulrica, a character who foretells a hero's murder in Giuseppe Verdi's opera *Un Ballo in Maschera* (A Masked Ball).

Carrag the Black by Don Maitz.

Healing

Sometimes witches use spells or potions to heal people. However, this is often done to trick someone. For example, the person might be healed, but only for a short time. Or, after they die, the healed person loses their soul. In the 1989 Disney movie *The Little Mermaid*, the witch makes Ariel a human for three days, but then Ariel must pay a terrible price.

Above: Ariel the mermaid with Ursula the sea witch in Disney's *The Little Mermaid*.

Telling the Future

Above: Modern-day tarot cards.

Witches often possess the ability to read the future in several different ways. Sometimes they drink a cup of tea, and then the leaves at the bottom of the cup reveal future events. Sometimes witches spread something on the ground, like dice, or the body parts of an animal. The witch then "reads" the placement of the objects, which tells them the future. Sometimes witches use a deck of cards called *tarot cards*. Each card that is revealed has a special significance, like death or love. In some cases, witches look into crystal balls and "see" events happening in the future.

Above: A fortune-teller uses tarot cards. A deck of tarot cards consists of 78 cards with five suits: swords, cups, coins, batons/wands, and a trump suit which consists of 22 symbolic cards showing figures and scenes. *Below:* A séance.

Conjuring up the Dead

Sometimes, witches can call on a person who has already died, which allows the deceased to speak. The most common method for this conjuring of the dead is at a séance, where a small group of people sit around a table and hold hands. The witch then invites the dead person into the room. The dead person then speaks, or is "channeled," through the witch.

Witch by Don Maitz.

Just Being Wicked

In most cases, witches are portrayed as evil people. In the story *Hansel and Gretel*, the children were lured to a gingerbread house and imprisoned so that the witch could eat them. A witch can't get much nastier than that. In Grimms' Fairy Tales' *Rapunzel*, a witch tricked a couple into giving up their daughter, and then kept the child locked up in a tall tower.

Witches are an ever-present part of fantasy literature. But how did the idea of witches start? Where did witchcraft come from? Who told the first stories about witches? To answer that question, we have to explore the Druids, a mysterious group of people who lived long ago.

Below: An 1892 Brothers Grimm book cover of *Hansel and Gretel.* Art by V.P. Mohn.

THE MYSTERIOUS DRUIDS

Facing Page: Crone by Don Maitz. *Below:* A part of the Gundestrup Cauldron.

Druids were a special group of people in Celtic society. The Celts were the people who lived in the British Isles, northern Europe, and Scandinavia for hundreds of years before the Roman invasion in 43 A.D. In the middle of Celtic society were the Druids. They were the best-educated people in the land. For the most part, the Druids ran the Celtic society. Druids included priests, judges, poets, and soothsayers. In those days, people thought that the Druids knew the future, or could read the future. Therefore, the people listened to the wisdom of the Druids.

Druids paid attention to the cycles of nature. They tried to get "in tune" with nature as much as possible. They held religious ceremonies in oak groves because they believed the spirit of the trees gave their ceremonies more power. They used plants that they believed had healing properties, like mistletoe. The Druids could tell their people when the best time was to plant crops, and when to harvest. They also claimed to be able to tell the future, and advised military leaders on the best times to go to war.

Unfortunately, the Druids didn't leave a written record. Their spells, their chants, their songs—very little has survived. So, archeologists and historians have to piece together bits of information from many places in order to understand the Druids. For example, archeologists have discovered a 2,000-year-old silver pot called the Gundestrup Cauldron. It was found in a peat bog in Denmark. It's the kind of pot you can imagine witches or wizards using to stir up batches of magical potions. Archaeologists think the cauldron was used for many years before being put in the bog as a kind of sacrifice. There are carvings on the cauldron that show horned gods and half-human, half-animal figures. There are also scenes that may depict human sacrifices.

Another example of archeology helping us to understand the Druids comes from a discovery called the Tollund Man. In 1950, a body was found in another Danish peat bog. The body was remarkably well preserved because the peat bog kills the bacteria that helps bodies decompose. It was so well preserved that the discoverers called the police, thinking it was a murder.

The Tollund Man, as he came to be called, may have been ritually sacrificed in a Druid ceremony. Scientists were able to look at the contents of his stomach to determine his last meal, which was some kind of stew or soup. The soup had many types of grains in it, but the grains did not come from the area. This leads scientists to believe that the grains were brought in for a special purpose, such as a ritual or ceremony. Scientists also found traces of ergot, which is a toxic mold found on rye grain. One of the side effects of ergot is that people have hallucinations—they see things that aren't there. Druids used ergot to induce trances and hallucinations. After his final meal, Tollund Man was strangled to death, then laid to rest in the bog. In the last 50 years, other preserved bodies have been discovered in Denmark, Germany, Ireland, and Britain.

Right: The Tollund Man lived around 400-300 B.C. The well-preserved body was found in a peat bog in Aarhus, Denmark, in 1950. A noose was still around his neck, indicating that he met a violent death. However, the body was carefully positioned in a curled, restful pose, which means he may have been part of a ritual Druid ceremony.

Above: A reenactment of a gathering of Druids at Stonehenge near Wiltshire, England.

In 43 A.D., the Romans invaded Britain, and then occupied it until about 400 A.D. The Romans limited the control Druids had over people. The Romans tolerated the Druids, but didn't think much of them. The Romans thought of themselves as the only civilized people, and everyone else—including the Druids—were barbarians. Historians believe that the Druids sometimes practiced human sacrifice. But many sources claim that, on the whole, the Druids were actually a peaceful people who were constantly in touch with nature.

In about 400 A.D., the Romans lost control of Britain. Many people revived the old Druid practices, which had been handed down from generation to generation. The historical King Arthur rose about this time in history. It makes sense that he may have had an adviser who was skilled in the old Druid ways of telling the future and harnessing the forces of nature. Some think the fictional wizard Merlin may have been a Druid.

SHAMANS

Druids weren't the first people to try to get in tune with nature and harness its magical powers. A very ancient form of magic called shamanism existed even before the Druids. In the time before science and civilization, the forces of nature could be terrifying. Tornados, blizzards, storms—nature could be deadly to those who didn't pay attention. By being aware of the rhythms of the seasons, people knew when they had to prepare for winter. By finding shelter when dark storm clouds were present, lives could be saved. Pre-civilized people began to understand which plants were good for food, and which ones were poisonous. They began to understand that some plants could be used as medicines. This kind of nature knowledge helped keep primitive tribes alive. People with this special knowledge of nature were called shamans, and they were revered as magicians. These were the earliest forms of wizards. There is archaeological evidence of shamanism reaching back 40,000 years.

Below: Bear's Belly, a North American Arikara medicine man, in a 1908 photo by Edward Curtis.

Shamans were animists. Animism is the belief that plants and animals have a spirit, just like humans. For an animist, the world is filled with spirits, which can be communicated with using the proper techniques. Spirits can reveal wisdom and knowledge about the world.

Shamans believed that they could cross over from the physical world to the spirit world. They did this by first going into a deep trance. The trance was achieved by either denying themselves food for a long time (fasting), or by chanting and dancing, which was often accompanied by rhythmic drumming. In many cases special medicines were given to help the shamans get into the trance state.

Above: Tzaramenda Naychapi, a modern shaman from Equador, South America.

When the shamans were in a trance, they were able to travel into the mystical world. Once there, shamans could talk with spirits and animals. When the trance was over, the shamans could tell "spirit stories" to eager members of the tribe.

Shamans were especially valuable to ancient hunting societies. Because they were so in tune with nature, they understood animal migratory routes. Shamans knew where prey was likely to be found during any time of the year. Because they were so good at locating animals, it was said that shamans could also make animals appear at certain times. When tribes survived based on their hunting success, shamans were very valuable and necessary.

Shamans were experts with plants and herbs. They knew which plants could lessen pain, and which ones could make trances. They knew which plants would create hallucinations or calm people down. Because they understood plants and herbs, they were able to create medical treatments. These medicines ranged from simple painkillers to drugs that helped the mentally ill. Even today, many of the medicines we use are from plants.

Shamanism was probably practiced in ancient societies all over the world. Evidence of their magical practice has been found as far away as Australia and the Arctic. In some places, for example Siberia and Mongolia, shamanism is still practiced today.

The ancient Shaman practice of communicating with nature, with animals especially, can be seen in today's fictional wizards, from Merlin to Harry Potter.

Left: A shaman of the Shortsy nation in Russia's Siberian Kemerovo region.

Below: Women convicted of being witches are burned.

WITCHES IN THE MIDDLE AGES

After the Roman Empire collapsed in about 400 A.D., Christianity began to take hold in Britain and the rest of northern Europe. Christian leaders tried to stop the practice of shamanism and other pagan (non-Christian) religions. By about 1000 A.D., Druids and their knowledge of magic were almost gone. Some Druids practiced in secret, but most of the old ways died out, along with the remaining few Druids.

One isolated group of people—witches—kept the old traditions alive. Witches had been around for centuries, even as far back as prehistoric times. Like shamans, witches used their knowledge of the natural world to help hunters find their prey. They were also skilled at concocting spells and magic potions, and telling the future. The ancient Greeks and Romans tolerated witches in their societies. It was the Romans who first made a distinction between good magic and bad magic. Witches who practiced bad magic were punished.

Witch Town by Don Maitz. The mandrake root, used in many witches' brews and medicines, sometimes produces the sensation of flying. This may be why witches have often been illustrated swooping across the night sky riding broomsticks or creatures

Once Christianity took hold in Europe, the dividing line between good and bad sorcery was erased. All witches were considered to be worshipers of the devil. In keeping the old Druid magic alive, most witches had to stay in hiding. Potions and spells were not written down out of fear of being caught. Knowledge was passed down orally from one generation of witches to the next.

The witches' knowledge of herbal remedies and potions became quite extensive. Many herbs and plants were boiled in large cauldrons. Witches learned their craft after many years of practice. They had to be careful: one bad recipe could easily prove fatal.

Like the shamans and Druids, witches used special medicines to help them fall into trances, which they believed allowed them to communicate with the spirit world.

One of the witches' favorite trance drugs was made from mandrake, a plant of the deadly nightshade family. The plant's unusually shaped roots gives it the resemblance of a human face or body. And, as if that isn't creepy enough, folklore says that mandrakes scream when pulled from the ground. Mandrake use is so common in witchcraft that they even make an appearance in the Harry Potter books.

Above: A photo of a mandrake root.
Below: A 16th-century illustration of a mandrake, with the long taproot resembling a man. It was believed that the root would scream when pulled from the ground, deafening the collector.

When mandrakes were converted into an ointment and spread on the body, a witch went into a trance-like state, accompanied by double vision and hallucinations. One common side effect of mandrake poisoning is the sensation of flying. This might be the reason why witches today are often shown flying through the air on their broomsticks. It is a piece of folklore that may have come down from the use of the mandrake plant.

As witches experimented more and more with herbs, they discovered many medicinal uses for their concoctions. Their hallucinogenic drugs may have been used as a primitive anesthesia for people who were in a lot of pain. There were also many herbal remedies that acted as painkillers, or helped wounds heal quicker. The witches' knowledge of medicines and natural healing was quite extensive for their time. Even today, modern drug companies are experimenting with long-lost witches brews, including mandrakes, in the hope of discovering new treatments for diseases such as cancer.

Witches have suffered at the hands of religious authorities down through the Middle Ages. After Christianity took hold in Europe, witches were often persecuted for being devil worshipers. European witch-hunts, especially in the late 1500s and 1600s, found many people falsely accused of witchcraft and devil worship. During this period of hysteria, many women were sent to prison, tortured, executed, or banished from society.

Above: A scene from 1993's *Hocus Pocus.* Bette Midler and Kathy Najimy play two classic witches.

Above: The Duckingstool by Charles Stanley Reinhart. This device, also called a diving chair, was sometimes used to punish witches. Strapped into the seat, the person was dunked into a nearby river or pond. The accused often drowned or died from the shock of the cold water.

The most famous case of "witchcraft hysteria" in the United States erupted in Salem, Massachusetts, beginning in 1692. Two girls developed fits, threw things, contorted their bodies, and had other strange symptoms. They were accused of being "bewitched." It wasn't long before many people in Salem were accusing many other people of witchcraft. The problem was that any kind of illness or death could be attributed to witchcraft, and the "victim" could file a complaint with the authorities. If a farmer's cow wandered away, the farmer could accuse someone of witchcraft. People began to accuse each other, and soon more than 150 people were imprisoned for the crime of witchcraft. About 19 men and women were hanged for being witches. The accusations continued until 1693, when a local pastor, Rev. Francis Dane, boldly spoke out, demanding that the trials and accusations stop. Dane said that it was better that 10 witches go free than one innocent person be put to death. This was very true for Pastor Dane, because some of his own family members were accused of being witches. Most historians believe the victims in Salem were falsely accused. Doctors today think the two girls who started it all suffered from some kind of medical condition.

Above: A witch trial. Punishment for those found guilty of witchcraft was often death.

MODERN-DAY WITCHES

During the 20th century, several writers revived an interest in witchcraft and ancient religious rituals. Modern witchcraft, often called Wicca, or The Craft, is a mix of the old ways plus elements of Goddess-worshiping religions and other pre-Christian beliefs. Some witches today claim they have an unbroken line of teaching from pre-Christian witchcraft, although this is impossible to prove.

Still, Wicca has a strong following today, and is considered by some to be a legitimate religion. There is not a single governing leadership of Wicca, and so beliefs and practices vary from place to place. Many are drawn to the practice because of its potential for spiritual growth, and because of its reverence of the natural world. Modern witches do not practice Satanism. They insist that they create magic only for good purposes, such as love potions or healing spells. Still, many conservative religions reject Wicca's standing as a formal religion, and insist that it is a pagan practice with roots in the worship of evil powers.

The literature of witches and wizards goes back hundreds, if not thousands, of years. Today, in the age of science, it's easy to think we have no more use for these mystical users of magic. But our popular culture is still filled with witches riding broomsticks and wizards casting astonishing spells. Stories of witches have been with us a long time, and will continue to be with us. After all, it's a whole lot easier for us to blame our misfortune on a witch's curse. When something bad happens, it's harder for us to blame random chance or our own poor judgment.

Below: A modern-day Wiccan, Fiona Horne, starred in the Sci Fi Channel's 2004 reality show *Mad Mad House.*

Above: Even in modern times, people are interested in witchcraft.

To many people, the world can be a complex, frightening place. Many of us often feel powerless to control events. Perhaps we're drawn to stories of wizards and witches because they help us make sense of the world, giving us a belief that we can control our future and our fears.

 GLOSSARY

ANIMISM

A belief in the existence of spirits and demons. Animists believe that all life is created by spiritual force. They believe that all natural things, like animals, trees, or even stones, have a spirit. Animists believe that these spirits can be communicated with, if one uses the proper technique. Mystical priests called shamans were part of animist societies, and claimed to talk to the spirits of the natural world.

BARBARIAN

A term used in the Middle Ages for anyone who didn't belong to one of the "great" civilizations such as the Greeks or Romans, or from the Christian kingdoms such as France or Britain.

CAULDRON

A large metal pot, with a lid and handle, used to cook food over an open fire. Cauldrons are often a convenient kind of pot in which to mix magic potions.

CELTIC

Refers to the people or the language of the Celts, who dominated the British Isles and parts of France and Scandinavia for hundreds of years before the Roman invasion and occupation of 43 A.D.

ERGOT

A reddish-brown or black fungus that attacks certain cereal grains, especially rye. Medicines called alkaloids can be extracted from this toxic mold. Druids used ergot to bring about visions and hallucinations.

FOLKLORE

The unwritten traditions, legends, and customs of a culture. Folklore is usually passed down by word of mouth from generation to generation.

HALLUCINATION

The perception of a sight or sound that isn't actually there. Hallucinations can occur because of mental illness, or be induced by certain medicines. Druids and witches used medicines to bring on hallucinations in order to contact what they believed to be the spirit world.

MIDDLE AGES

In European history, a period defined by historians as between 476 A.D. and 1450 A.D.

MISTLETOE

A parasitic evergreen plant that grows on deciduous or evergreen trees. Mistletoe has yellow-green leaves, yellow flowers, and white poisonous berries. Sprigs of mistletoe are hung at Christmas as decorations. Druids used the plant to make medicines.

ORAL

Communicating by using spoken language. Most folklore is passed down from generation to generation by oral tradition. This means the stories are spoken and remembered, not written down.

PAGAN

Generally, a person who doesn't practice a widely recognized formal religion, such as Christianity, Judaism, or Islam. There are several definitions of the word pagan. In the context of this book, pagans are people who worship nature or the earth, such as druids or witches.

SHAMAN

A person who performs an ancient form of magic called shamanism. They used a special knowledge of nature to help their tribes. Shamans believed they could heal, communicate with plans and animals, and walk between this world and the mystical world. Shamans often went into deep trances to perform their magic. There is archaeological evidence of shamanism reaching back 40,000 years.

TRANCE

A kind of hypnotic mental state. A person in a trance doesn't seem to be affected by interruptions from the outside world. Instead, he seems to be intensely concentrating on something, sometimes chanting phrases over and over.

Witchcraft
by Don Maitz.

INDEX

A

anesthesia 24
animist 16
archeologist 12
archeology 14, 16
Arctic 19
Ariel 9
Arthur, King 15
Australia 19

B

bacteria 14
barbarian 15
bewitch 26
black magic 4
Britain 14, 15, 21
British Isles 12

C

cancer 24
cauldron 4, 12, 24
Celts 12
channel 9
chant 12, 16
Christianity 21, 24, 25
Craft, The 28
crystal ball 9
curse 4, 6, 28

D

dance 16
Dane, Francis 26
demon 6
Denmark 12, 14
devil 6, 24, 25
Disney 9
Druids 4, 11, 12, 14, 15, 16, 21, 24

E

ergot 14
Europe 12, 21, 24, 25
evil 4, 6, 11, 28

F

fantasy 11
fasting 16
future 4, 9, 12, 15, 21, 29

G

Germany 14
Greek 21
Grimms' Fairy Tales 11
Gundestrup Cauldron 12
gypsies 6

H

hallucination 14, 19, 24
Hansel and Gretel 11
healing 9
herb 19, 24
historians 12, 15, 26
human 9, 24

I

Ireland 14

L

Little Mermaid, The 9

M

Macbeth 4
magic 6, 16, 21, 24, 28
magician 16
mandrake 24
Massachusetts 26
medicine 16, 19, 24
Merlin 15, 19
Middle Ages 4, 25
mistletoe 12
Mongolia 19

N

nature 12, 15, 16, 19

P

pagan 21, 28
peat bog 12, 14
plants 19, 24
poison 16
potion 6, 9, 12, 21, 24, 28
Potter, Harry 19, 24

R

Rapunzel 11
remedy 24
Roma 6
Roman 12, 15, 21

S

sacrifice 12, 14, 15
Salem, MA 26
Satanism 28
Scandinavia 12
séance 9
Shakespeare, William 4
shaman 4, 16, 19, 21, 24
shamanism 16, 18, 21

Siberia 19
Snow White 6
song 12
sorcery 24
spell 6, 9, 12, 21, 24, 28
spirit 12, 16, 19, 24
spirit stories 19

T

tarot cards 9
Tollund Man 14
torture 25
trance 14, 16, 19, 24

U

United States 26

W

warlock 4
warts 4
white magic 4
Wicca 28
witchcraft 11, 24, 25, 26, 28
wizard 4, 12, 15, 16, 19, 28, 29
Wizard of Oz, The 4

Above: Mexican Sorcerer by Don Maitz.